MW00652763

This Child

Words Of
St. Thérèse Of Lisieux
With
Reflections and Prayers

This Child

Words of
St. Thérèse of Lisieux
With
Reflections and Prayers

Text
James Grundl

Illustrations
Sister Mary Joseph, O.C.D.

Carmel of Port Tobacco

Published by   Carmel of Port Tobacco
                   5678 Mt. Carmel Road
                   La Plata, MD 20646, USA
                   www.carmelofporttobacco.com

Library of Congress Control Number: 2003111409
ISBN: 0-9743914-0-9

Printed in the United States of America by Print4Less.com

CONTENTS

Preface

Thérèse wrote the story of her life spontaneously, hurriedly. She once remarked, "It is like fishing with a line, I write whatever comes to the end of my pen." The words so hastily put down in a little copybook describe an adventure of spiritual discovery that for a century has attracted the minds and hearts of the most common and uncommon of God's people on earth. With imagination, wit, and candor, the Child of the Child Jesus lived and taught the boundless mercy of God and His thirst for love. For those who would be God's love but are little and weak, she advocates a realistic spiritual revolution: The Little Way of Spiritual Childhood. It is her own path of total abandonment to God and unshakable confidence in the folly of His love.

As a victim of love driven by intense desires and toughened by a persistent trial of faith, Thérèse would have everyone know the joy and peace of joining suffering with love, of accepting each sacrifice that comes to us in the tangle of everyday living. She tells us, "Love consumes everything. . .it leaves nothing but a humble and profound peace." This is the foundation of her bold and accessible spirituality.

The words of St. Thérèse are taken from *Story of a Soul* (1996) and *Her Last Conversations* (1977) in the translation by John Clarke.O.C.D published by the Institute of Carmelite Studies. They are accompanied by reflections and prayers composed annually as Feast Day Pieces by a nuclear scientist who has been deeply influenced and endlessly fascinated by the famous child of Lisieux. The illustrations are the work of a Discalced Carmelite, artist and founder of the Monastery of St. Joseph located in Port Tobacco, Maryland, the site of the first foundation of religious women in the United States.

The location of each excerpt is given as an abbreviation (SS or LC) followed by a page number. Archive photographs of St. Thérèse are from the Office Central de Lisieux, France.

She shines brightly among the little ones to whom the secrets of the Kingdom were revealed in a most special way.

Thérèse possesses an exceptional universality. Her person, the Gospel message of the "little way" of trust and spiritual childhood have received and continue to receive a remarkable welcome, which has transcended every border.

— John Paul II

It's Like

Fishing

With A Line

IMAGINE!

God will sip you like a drop of dew,
    she said;
We'll both rest on God's two knees;
    she said,
Oh, you'll see, it will be like a shower of roses.

> SHE REJOICED IN LIGHT
> SHE REJOICED IN DARKNESS
> SHE REJOICED IN CONFIDENCE

I'm little, I work only for his pleasure, his whims;
    she said,
My desire is to be unpetalled forever,
To love, to return to make love loved.

> SHE REJOICED IN LIGHT
> SHE REJOICED IN DARKNESS
> SHE REJOICED IN INNOCENCE

The chalice is full. . .full to the brim,
    she said;
The blackness of night is in my soul!
    she said,
I sing only of what I want to believe.

> SHE REJOICED IN LIGHT
> SHE REJOICED IN DARKNESS
> SHE REJOICED IN DESOLATION

What I need is the fire of love;
  she said,
My God, my God, have pity on me!
All right! I wouldn't want to suffer less.

    SHE REJOICED IN LIGHT
    SHE REJOICED IN DARKNESS
    SHE REJOICED UNAFRAID

When I'm in heaven, I'll begin my mission,
  she said;
I tell you, I will die with my weapons in my hands;
  she said,
I say nothing to him, I love him.

    SHE REJOICED IN LIGHT
    SHE REJOICED IN DARKNESS
    THÉRÈSE, HELP US REJOICE

WORDS OF THÉRÈSE — I

I shall begin to sing what I must sing eternally: "The Mercies of the Lord."
SS-13

It seems to me that if a little flower could speak, it would tell simply what God has done for it without trying to hide its blessings. It would not say in false humility, it is not beautiful or without perfume, that the sun has taken away its splendor and the storm has broken its stem when it knows that all this is untrue.
SS-15

The flower. . .rejoices at the totally gratuitous gifts of Jesus. She knows that nothing in herself was capable of attracting the divine glances and His mercy alone brought about everything that is good in her.
SS-15

All the great truths of religion, the mysteries of eternity, plunged my soul into a state of joy not of this earth. I experienced what God reserved for those who love Him.
SS-102

I wondered for a long time why God has preferences, why all souls do not receive an equal amount of graces. I was puzzled at seeing how our Lord was pleased to caress certain ones from the cradle to the grave. . . . I wondered why poor savages died in great numbers without even having heard the name of God pronounced. Jesus deigned to teach me this mystery by setting before me the book of nature; . . . He willed to create great souls comparable to lilies and roses, but He also created smaller ones and these must be content to be daisies or violets destined to give joy to God's glances when He looks down at His feet. . . . God does not call those who are worthy, but those whom He pleases.   SS-13/14

. . .for me to translate my thoughts, I have to be *like the solitary sparrow*, and this is rarely my lot. When I begin to take up my pen, behold a Sister passes by, a pitchfork on her shoulder. She believes she will distract me with a little idle chatter, . . .then another hay worker throws flowers on my lap, perhaps believing this will inspire me with poetic thoughts. I. . .would prefer to see the flowers remain swaying on their stems. Finally, fatigued by opening and shutting this famous copybook, I . . .copy out some thoughts from the psalms. . .   SS-227

Sometimes I felt alone, very much alone. . . I repeated these words which always gave rise to a new peace and strength in my heart: "Life is your barque and not your home!" . . . Doesn't the Book of Wisdom say: "*Life is like a ship that plows the restless waves and leaves after it no trace of its rapid passage?*" When I think these things, my soul is plunged into infinity, and it seems to me it already touches the eternal shore.   SS-87

Ah! it is prayer, it is sacrifice which gives me all my strength; these are the invincible weapons which Jesus has given me. They can touch souls much better than words, as I have frequently experienced.   SS-241

THÉRÈSE OF LISIEUX

Child, you told us with your life
    That every human life
    Can have holiness of purpose.
Each surrender to love,
    However small or isolated
    However poorly understood
    However surrounded by failure,
Is a precious exchange with God.

COME AND SEE

You, who acknowledge the unsearchable ways of God,
    Who rest easily or anxiously in his expectant
        embrace;
You, who are touched only by the works of nature,
    Captivated, beguiled by the splendor and tumult.

Come, meet a child enthralled by nature,
    Inspired by the starry vault or by a lowly daisy;
A child wildly determined to catch God,
    To blaze a child's way to his fierce love.

Come, fathom an irrepressible spirit,
    In rich turns of words,
        in their reckless abandon,
In sharp wit alive to the minutiae of life,
    In anecdotes condensed in telling phrases.

Join the many who explore her singular enlightenment,
    Daylight for our stumblings, night light for our
        fears.
Doctor of the Church, now, but no less a youth,
    Excited to share her conquest of a caring God.

THIS CHILD

Born in a land of ancient churches:
Soaring vaults of ribbed stone,

    A FEARLESS INTIMATE OF GOD:
    HER NAME AMONG THE STARS,

Revelation in daring openings of light,
Stone upon stone, sentinels for his body,
A breathless call to silence, to prayer.

    HER SONG, "THE MERCIES OF THE LORD."
    "MY GOD, I CHOOSE ALL," SHE SAID.

WORDS OF THÉRÈSE — II

I am going to stammer some words even though I feel it is quite impossible for the human tongue to express things which the human heart can hardly understand.   SS-187

Jesus does not demand great actions from us, but simply *surrender* and *gratitude*.   SS-188

. . .if I had committed all possible crimes, I would always have the same confidence; I feel that this whole multitude of offenses would be like a drop of water thrown into a fiery furnace.   LC-89

. . .I do not have the courage to force myself to search out *beautiful* prayers in books. There are so many of them it really gives me a headache! . . .like children who do not know how to read, I say very simply to God what I wish to say. . . For me, . . .it is a simple glance directed to heaven, it is a cry of gratitude and love in the midst of trial as well as joy. . .   SS-242

. . .our humiliation at the moment is our glory later on, even in this life.   LC-117

Ah! the Lord is so good to me; it is quite impossible for me to fear Him.   SS-250

We who run in the way of love shouldn't be thinking of suffering that can take place in the future; it's a lack of confidence, it's like meddling in the work of creation.

LC-106

_____

I'm not breaking my head over the writing of my "little" life; it's as though I were fishing with a line: I write whatever comes to the end of my pen.   LC-63

I remember one day when the beautiful blue sky became suddenly overcast and soon the thunder began to roll and lightning flashed through the dark clouds. I saw it strike a short distance away, . . . I was thrilled with delight because God seemed so close!   SS-37

When we were on the way home, I would gaze upon the stars which were twinkling ever so peacefully in the skies and the sight carried me away. There was especially one cluster of *golden pearls* which attracted my attention and gave me great joy because they were in the form of a -T-. I pointed them out to Papa and told him my name was written in heaven.   SS-43

In the evening at that moment when the sun seems to bathe itself in the immensity of the ocean waves, leaving a *luminous trail* behind, I went and sat down on a huge rock with *Pauline*. . .I contemplated this luminous trail for a long time. It was to me the image of God's grace shedding its light across the path the little white-sailed vessel had to travel.   SS-48

13

Jesus was sleeping as usual in my little boat; ah! I see very well how rarely souls allow him to sleep peacefully within them. Jesus is so fatigued with always having to take the initiative and attend to others, He hastens to take advantage of the repose I offer to Him.   SS-165

At the time, I was having great interior trials of all kinds, even to the point of asking myself whether heaven really existed.   SS-173

Sometimes when my mind is in such great dryness that it is impossible to draw forth one single thought to unite me with God, I very slowly recite an "Our Father" and then the angelic salutation (to Mary). . . they nourish my soul much more than if I had recited them precipitately a hundred times.   SS-243

When I think of how much trouble I've had all my life trying to recite the rosary!   LC-160

Ah! how contrary are the teachings of Jesus to the feelings of nature! Without the help of His grace it would be impossible not only to put them into practice but to even understand them.   SS-229

A PRAYER

Child of Flowers,
   earthy simplicity
   blooms of wit
   showered with affection,
                MISTRESS OF WORDS
                COME AMONG US.

Child of Jesus,
   confidence unbounded
   bursts of imagination
   apple of his eye,
                MISTRESS OF THE WORD
                COME AMONG US.

Child of the Holy Face,
   gifted with innocence
   triumphant in struggles
   eager for his chalice,
                MISTRESS OF SUFFERING
                COME AMONG US.

Victim of love's holocaust,
   keep your promises, now,
   whenever our faith falters,
                HEAR, DO NOT FAIL US.

Help us surrender to God
   with the same obedience and trust,
   and passion you never denied him,
                HEAR, DO NOT FAIL US.

A

Weak

Little Bird

A White Flower

Bright blossom, tough stem.
Bauble for a Child, so small.
So close, a dark wall.

ABOVE ALL

This child confounds every urge
To shrug off the extravagance of the Gospel.

Her doctrine is layer upon layer of simplicity,
Saturated with intelligence, fired by scripture;

Her teaching, like a huge mobile, overwhelms
In its immediacy, in its natural balance and motion;

Her life, her message for the common Christian
Is a fresh sensuous display of transcendence.

WORDS OF THÉRÈSE — III

Jesus has no need of books or teachers to instruct souls;
He teaches without the noise of words. Never have I
heard Him speak, but. . .I find just when I need them
certain lights which I had not seen until then, and. . .these
are most abundant in the midst of my daily occupations.

SS-179

It is not to remain in a golden ciborium that He comes to
us *each day* from heaven, it's to find another heaven,
infinitely more dear to Him than the first: the heaven of
our soul, made to His image, the living temple of the
adorable Trinity!

SS-104

The Blessed Virgin. . .didn't have a Blessed Virgin to
love. And so this is one more sweetness for us and one
less sweetness for her!

LC-162

Ah! poor women, how they are misunderstood! And
yet they love God in much larger numbers than men do
and during the Passion of Our Lord, women had more
courage than the apostles since they braved the insults
of the soldiers and dared to dry the adorable face of
Jesus. It is undoubtedly because of this that He allows
misunderstanding to be their lot on earth, since He chose
it for Himself. In heaven He will show that His thoughts
are not men's thoughts, for then the *last will be first.*

SS-140

Mama told Marie to dress me in my Sky-blue frock with the lace trimmings but not to leave my arms bare lest the Sun burn them. I allowed myself to be dressed with the indifference a child of my age should really have, but I thought to myself that I would look much more pretty with my arms bare.   SS-24

Céline became the confidante of my thoughts. . . . Jesus . . .formed bonds in our hearts stronger than blood. He made us become *spiritual sisters*,. . . The sparks of love He sowed so generously in our souls, and the delicious and strong wine He gave us to drink made all passing things disappear before our eyes. . . With enraptured gaze we beheld. . .the bright stars twinkling in the deep skies, the light breath of the evening breeze making the snowy clouds float easily along; all this raised our souls to heaven, that beautiful heaven whose "obverse side" alone we were able to contemplate.   SS-103

I look upon myself as a *weak little bird*, with only light down as covering. . . . At times the little bird's heart is assailed by the storm, and it seems it should believe in the existence of no other thing except the clouds surrounding it. . . . It cries like a swallow and in its sweet song it recounts in detail all its infidelities, thinking in the boldness of its full trust that it will acquire in even greater fullness the love of *Him* who came to call not the just but sinners.
                                                            SS-198/199

. . .you can see that I am a *very little soul* and that I can offer God only *very little things*.   SS-250

22

THE LITTLE WAY

GENESIS
Are we not all on a little way,
    Jots, specks of creation who rest uneasy
    Among spiraling stars and violent dust?
Our precarious flesh, ghostless many say,
    Is it nought but twisted coils of that very dust?
Thérèse lived with this darkest of all fears,
    Heard the serpent's hiss of hopelessness.

EXODUS
Ever determined, the *little one* scrambled to Jesus.
    With an *immense desire* to be God's own,
    She explored his ancient promise of Merciful Love.
Exuberant words on cheap paper declare
    Moments of darkness and suffering are touches
        of that Love.
She found more: *weakness and littleness* accepted
    Are God's everlasting relish and delight.

LEGACY
A Little Way, very straight, very short,
A way of confidence in God's boundless *love*
    For *little ones* who are *weak* and imperfect.

A way of small steps and sudden tumbles,
A way to surrender the lonely I of self
    To him who longs to enrich our poverty.

A way to *pursue love* in the smallest affairs,
A way to bear stubborn storms of emotion
    That render prayer dry and mindless.

A way to lift daily discouragements into prayer,
A way of faithful desperation when fighting
    The cold assaults of unbelief.

A way to adopt the fearless innocence of a child,
A way to revel in the *dazzling reality* of the Eucharist,
    To be consumed by the Body of Christ.

For the courageous, a way to *plunge into the abyss
        of his LOVE* !
For all God's *Little Ones*, an adventure, a celebration,
    A way to rejoice in the *eagerness of his love!*

25

WORDS OF THÉRÈSE – IV

I always feel the same bold confidence of becoming a great saint because I don't count on my merits since I have none. . . God alone, content with my weak efforts, will raise me to Himself and make me a saint, clothing me in His infinite merits.   SS-72

To be little. . .is not to become discouraged over one's faults, for children fall often, but they are too little to hurt themselves very much.   LC-139

Ah! how good the Lord is in having matured my soul, and in having given it wings. All the nets of the hunters would not be able to frighten me, for". . .the net is spread in vain before the eyes of them that have wings." (Prov 1:17)   SS-224

. . . the Holy Spirit, before Jesus' birth, dictated this prophetic prayer: "Draw me, we shall run." What is it then to be "Drawn" if not to be united in an intimate way to the object which captivates our heart? . . . I ask Jesus to draw me into the flames of His love, to unite me so closely to Him that He live and act in me.   SS-257

But was it possible to come all the way to Rome and not go down into the Colosseum? For me it was impossible! . . . I saw what I was looking for and I cried to Céline: "Come quick! We can get through!" We crossed the barrier. . .we were climbing down over the ruins which rumbled under our feet. . .the guide . . .had pointed out a tiny bit of pavement marked with a cross as the place where the martyrs fought,. . . We soon found it and threw ourselves on our knees on this sacred soil. . . . My heart was beating hard when my lips touched the dust stained with the blood of the first Christians.   SS-130/131

I was in the laundry doing the washing in front of a sister who was throwing dirty water into my face every time she lifted the handkerchiefs to her bench; my first reaction was to draw back and wipe my face to show the sister . . . she would do me a favor to be more careful. But I immediately thought. . .it would be very foolish to refuse these treasures . . . and I took care not to show my struggle. I. . .was so successful that in the end I had really taken a liking to this kind of aspersion, and I promised myself to return another time to this nice place where one received so many treasures.   SS-250

If, when I am preparing for some work, I find that the brushes and the paints are in disorder, if a rule or a penknife has disappeared, patience is very close to abandoning me and I must take my courage in both hands in order to reclaim the missing object without bitterness.
SS-226

I just saw a little sparrow on the garden wall, waiting patiently for its parents; from time to time, it gave forth its little chirp, calling them to come and give it a mouthful of food. I thought it was like me.   LC-78

27

Jesus knew very well that His little flower stood in need of the living waters of humiliation, for she was too weak to take root without this kind of help, . . . the dew of humiliation (was) so delightful that she would be very careful not to exchange it for the insipid water of praise.

SS-206

My mortifications consisted in breaking my will, always so ready to impose itself on others, in holding back a reply, in rendering little services without any recognition, in not leaning my back against a support when seated.

SS-143

Ah! if God had not showered His beneficent rays upon His little flower, she could never have accustomed herself to earth, for she was too weak to stand up against the rains and the storms. She needed warmth, a gentle dew, and the springtime breezes. Never were these lacking. Jesus had her find them beneath the snow of trial!

SS-35

God made me feel that true glory is that which will last eternally, and to reach it, it isn't necessary to perform striking works but to hide oneself and practice virtue in such a way that the left hand knows not what the right is doing.

SS-72

Time is nothing in your eyes, and a single day is like a thousand years. You can, then, in one instant prepare me to appear before you.

SS-277

29

TITLED CHILD

Teach all,
> Who seek God but do not surrender,
> Who avoid the healing waters of humiliation,
> Who know not the peace of suffering with love.

Teach all,
> Who are lonely in earth's tangled spaces,
> Who probe and ponder every crossing and crevice,
> Who explore with busy hands and facile tongues.

Teach all,
> Who are disjoined from a caring God,
> Who do not pray in their desert of unbelief,
> Who have not the courage to become children.

Teach,
> With your passion for truth and earthy realities,
> With your natural wit and sharp nuggets from
>   scripture,
> With your bright, extravagant webs of imagination.

Teach,
> From your own experience of unbelief,
> Your readiness to eat the dark bread of trial,
> And so to bring the flame of faith to sinners.

Teach,
> With your Little Way of Spiritual Childhood:
> The tireless pursuit of love in small happenings,
> And unshakable trust in the folly of God's love.

My

Vocation

Is Love

"MY VOCATION IS LOVE"
--A CANTICLE

Jesus confides in me,
    in secret he teaches me,
Marvels of the law of love
    he reveals to me.

My tongue stammers, my heart
    can hardly understand:
All can be all
    in the path of love.

To the boundless desires of my soul,
    Love descends –
My foolishness, my weakness, my nothingness
    is transformed into fire.

Love has chosen me,
    imperfect creature,
To be love's flame,
    love's victim.

Come, whoever is little,
    surrender to love,
Know that love is repaid
    with love alone.

THIRST

You flew high bold chickadee.

Like none other from saints or sinners, your words
    penetrate reality with the guileless wisdom of a
        child,
    with images daring beyond the catch of reason.
Attached to scripture like the dress of leaves to a tree,
    they reveal the persistent quest of a caring God.

Your words tumble out, unquenchably sure,
    alive to earth but anxious for God's touch.
Simple, intense, contoured like classic sculpture,
    they call out to us, obsessed masters of nature,
    giddy revelers who ignore the deep of creation.

They tell of thirsts that abide in every thirst–
    our thirst, to find, to know, to taste love,
    God's thirst, to be that taste.
Read in trenches of mud and blood, your words
    touch little souls, learned souls, mission souls,
        everywhere.

Speak to us Child of Jesus, now, on high!

WORDS OF THÉRÈSE – V

The little flower transplanted to Mount Carmel was to expand under the shadow of the cross. The tears and blood of Jesus were to be her dew, and her Sun was His adorable face veiled with tears.   SS-151

These words of Isaiah. . ."There is no beauty in Him, no comeliness etc.,". . .(are) the whole foundation of my devotion to the Holy Face, or to express it better, the foundation of all my piety. I, too, have desired to be without beauty, alone in treading the winepress, unknown to everyone.   LC-135

Your little bird. . .wants to be fascinated by Your divine glance. It wants to become the prey of your love. One day I hope that. . .you will plunge it for all eternity into the burning Abyss of this Love to which it has offered itself as victim.   SS-200

Just as a torrent, throwing itself impetuously into the ocean, drags after it everything it encounters in its passage, in the same way, O Jesus, the soul who plunges into the shoreless ocean of Your Love, draws with it all the treasures it possesses.   SS-254

I should be desolate for having slept (for seven years) during my hours of prayer and my thanksgiving after Holy Communion; well, I am not desolate. I remember that little children are as pleasing to their parents when they are asleep as well as when they are wide awake. . . I remember that: *"The Lord knows our weakness, that He is mindful that we are but dust and ashes."* SS-165

There is in the community a sister who has the faculty of displeasing me in everything, . . . for this Sister who gave me so many struggles, I took care to render her all the services possible. . .(including) my most friendly smile . . .One day at recreation she asked: ". . .what attracts you so much towards me; every time you look at me, I see you smile?" Ah! what attracted me was Jesus hidden in the depths of her soul. . . SS-222/223

Jesus . . . has no need of our works but only of our *love*, . . . He did not fear to *beg* for a little water from the Samaritan woman. He was thirsty. But when He said: *"Give me to drink,"* it was the *love* of His poor creature the creator of the universe was seeking. He was thirsty for love. SS-189

How sweet is the way of *love*. True, one can fall or commit infidelities, but, knowing *how to draw profit from everything,* love quickly consumes everything that can be displeasing to Jesus; it leaves nothing but a humble and profound peace in the depths of the heart. SS-179

I am only a child, powerless and weak, and yet it is my weakness that gives me the boldness of offering myself as VICTIM of Your Love, O Jesus! . . .me, a weak and imperfect creature. Is not this choice worthy of *Love?* Yes, in order that Love be fully satisfied, it is necessary that It lower Itself, and that It lower Itself to nothingness and transform this nothingness into *fire.* SS-195

WERE YOU WATCHING?

Thérèse, was your exuberant spirit
>   With sandaled Carmelites tossing rose petals,
>   With stalwarts carrying the heavy reliquary,
>   In the midst of patient crowds, so quiet,
>   In long lines, long past midnight?

Thérèse, did you smile to see
>   Wheelchairs and blue jeans in crowded chapel
>   doorways,
>   Cold feet fidgeting on cold sidewalks,
>   Toddlers held up to catch a glimpse,
>   Outstretched arms over bowed heads,
>   Tiny fingers, rosaries in wrinkled hands,
>   Reaching to touch the cover of your traveling
>   bones?

Thérèse, were you able to hear:
>   *A place of peace, it's incredible. . . I feel her presence*
>   *It's an honor. . . it's an extension of heaven*
>   *A good saint. . . and a very good writer*
>   *In struggles and suffering. . . fragile as we are fragile*
>   *We have always loved her. . . she was quite a gal*
>   *My Dad never cries. . . Is the box magic?*

Thérèse, missionary to a confused world,
Surely you were excited when thousands came,
Drawn by your daring impetuous promise to return.

SIMPLY AWESOME a bold headline declared.

DEEP, THIS CHALLENGE TO DISCONNECTED MODERNITY!

WORDS OF THÉRÈSE – VI

Because I was little and weak, He lowered Himself to me, He instructed me secretly in the things of His love.

SS-105

The science of love, ah, yes, this word resounds sweetly in the ear of my soul, and I desire only this science. . . . I understand so well that it is only love which makes us acceptable to God and this love is my only ambition. Jesus deigned to show me the road that leads to the Divine Furnace, and this road is the *surrender* of the little child who sleeps without fear in its Father's arms.

SS-187/188

I would like to enlighten souls as did the *Prophets* and the *Doctors*. I have the *vocation of the Apostle*. I would like to travel over the whole earth to preach Your Name. . . But *O my Beloved*, one mission alone would not be sufficient for me, I would want to preach the gospel on all the five continents. . . I would be a missionary, not for a few years only but from the beginning of creation until the consummation of the ages.

SS-192/193

Are my measureless desires only but a dream, a folly? Ah! if this be so, Jesus, then enlighten me, for you know I am seeking only the truth. If my desires are rash, then make them disappear. . .

SS-197

Jesus, I cannot fathom the depths of. . .my bold desires. My excuse is that I am a *child*. . . . But how will she prove her *love* since *love* is proved by works? Well, the little child *will strew flowers*. . .not allowing one little sacrifice to escape, not one look, not one word, profiting by all the smallest things and doing them through love. . . . I shall sing, for could one cry while doing such a joyous action? I shall sing even when I must gather my flowers in the midst of thorns. . . .   SS-196

Ah! my Jesus, pardon me if. . .my desires and longings reach even unto infinity. . . . I feel within me the *vocation* of the WARRIOR, THE PRIEST, THE APOSTLE, THE DOCTOR, THE MARTYR. . .O Jesus, my love, my life, how can I combine these contrasts? How can I realize the desires of my poor *little* soul?   SS-192

I feel it more than ever before, Jesus is *parched*, for He meets only the ungrateful and indifferent among His disciples in the world, and among *His own disciples*, alas, He finds few hearts who surrender to Him without reservations, who understand the real tenderness of His infinite Love.   SS-189

Is Your disdained Love to remain closed up within Your Heart? . . . It seems to me You would be happy not to hold back the waves of infinite tenderness within You. If Your justice loves to release itself,. . .how much more does Your Merciful Love desire to *set souls on fire*. . . .O my Jesus let me be this happy victim; consume Your holocaust with the fire of Your Divine Love.   SS-181

41

I finally had rest. . . . If the Church had a body composed of different members, the most necessary and most noble of all could not be lacking to it, and so I understood that the Church had a heart and this heart was BURNING WITH LOVE. . . . I understood that LOVE COMPRISED ALL VOCATIONS, THAT LOVE WAS EVERYTHING THAT IT EMBRACED ALL TIMES AND PLACES. . .IN A WORD THAT IT WAS ETERNAL!   SS-194

Then, in the excess of my delirious joy, I cried out: O Jesus, my Love. . . .my vocation, at last I have found it . . .MY VOCATION IS LOVE! . . . In the heart of the Church, my Mother, I shall be Love. Thus I shall be everything, and thus my dream will be realized. SS-194

Why speak of a delirious joy? No, this expression is not exact, for it was rather the calm and serene peace of the navigator perceiving the beacon which must lead him to the port . . . O luminous Beacon of love, I know how to reach You, I have found the secret of possessing Your flame.   SS-195

In order to live in one single act of perfect love, I OFFER MYSELF AS A VICTIM OF HOLOCAUST TO YOUR MERCIFUL LOVE, asking You to consume me incessantly, allow the waves of infinite tenderness, shut up within You, to overflow into my soul. . .I want, O my Beloved, at each beat of my heart to renew this offering to You an infinite number of times, until the shadows having disappeared I may be able to tell You of my Love in an Eternal Face to Face!   SS-277

A PETITION IN DARKNESS

Virgin Child of Lisieux,
    champion of confidence, reach out,
Touch my troubled soul,
    speak softly to my distress.

Hear the cry of a pilgrim
    alone on a darkening road,
Where clouds like those you knew
    hide the Sun of Life.

The clamor of rebellion is everywhere,
    ceaseless are the sounds of impudence;
The living deny life,
    the God-fearing cannot be heard.

Child of the Child Jesus,
    help me surrender to the Lord,
To walk joyfully in His presence,
    to rest unshaken in the darkness.

CHANT TO ST. THÉRÈSE

Daughter of Normandy's wealth,
Bright confident maid,
Architect of the Little Way,
                    PRAY FOR US

Child of the Child Jesus,
Spouse of Christ crucified,
Victim of consuming love,
                    PRAY FOR US

Toughened by the fire of doubt,
Ravaged by your own blood,
Intimate of God's darkness,
                    REMEMBER US

I'm

A Litttle

Seed

A LITANY FOR
ST. THÉRÈSE'S DAY

This Child of courageous desires
This Child of exquisite extravagance

> Maid of intelligence
> Virgin most sensible
> Daughter of Wisdom
> > PRAY FOR US
> Plaything of God
> Unafraid in shadows
> Chickadee among eagles
> > TEACH US YOUR WAY

This Child of the Little Way
This Child of sober truth

> Champion of our worth in small struggles
> Inspired by weakness, untouched by failure
> Apostle of simplicity and boundless trust
> > TEACH US CONFIDENCE

> Warrior of love laden with affection
> Will of steel, passion for surrender
> Victim of love, possessed by God
> > PRAY FOR US

Blooms of suffering cultivated in darkness,
Alone in agony, death by suffocation,
Her last words, wonders of spirit,
A storm of glory, this child!

Abandonment
Glistening snowflake,
Shafts of sunlight break
                    thick clouds,
Unafraid it melts.

WORDS OF THÉRÈSE – VII

The little bird wills *to fly* towards the bright Sun which attracts its eye, imitating its brothers, the eagles, whom it sees climbing up towards the Divine Furnace of the Holy Trinity. But, alas, the only thing it can do is *raise its little wings*; to *fly* is not within its *little* power.   SS-198

One Sunday, looking at a picture of Our Lord on the cross, I was struck by the blood flowing from one of His divine hands. . .I resolved to remain in spirit at the foot of the cross and receive this divine dew. I understood then, I was to pour it out upon souls. The cry of Jesus on the cross sounded continually in my heart: "I Thirst!" These words ignited within me an unknown and very living fire.   SS-99

I desired that, like the face of Jesus, "my face be truly hidden, that no one on earth would know me." I thirsted after suffering, I longed to be forgotten.   SS-152

He permitted my soul to be invaded by the thickest darkness, and the thought of heaven. . .no longer anything but the cause of struggle and torment. This trial was to last not a few days or a few weeks, it was not to be extinguished until the hour set by God Himself and this hour has not yet come.   SS-211

It's the reasoning of the worst materialists which is imposed upon my mind: Later, unceasingly making new advances, science will explain everything naturally; we shall have the absolute reason for everything that exists. . . . In spite of this trial which has taken away *all my joy*, I nevertheless cry out: "*You have given me DELIGHT, O Lord, in ALL your doings."*

LC-257 /SS-214

. . .faith . . .is no longer a veil for me, it is a wall which reaches right up to the heavens and covers the starry firmament. When I sing of the happiness of heaven and of the eternal possession of God, I feel no joy in this, for I sing simply of what I WANT TO BELIEVE.

SS-214

It is true that at times a very small ray of the sun comes to illumine my darkness, and then the trial ceases for an instant, but afterwards. . .the fog which surrounds me becomes more dense; it penetrates my soul and envelops it in such a way that it is impossible to discover within it the sweet image of my Fatherland; everything has disappeared!

SS-214 /213

O Jesus, why can't I tell all *little souls* how unspeakable is Your condescension? . . .Your secrets of Love, O Jesus. . .can You not reveal them to others? . . .I beg You to do it. I beg You to cast Your Divine Glance upon a great number of *little* souls. I beg You to choose a legion of *little* Victims worthy of Your LOVE!

SS-200

. . .I can't rest as long as there are souls to be saved. But when the angel will have said; "Time is no more!" then I will take my rest. . . .

LC-102

...THE HOLY FACE

I.

Long ago I saw your face,
    near as the surrounding darkness,
    so close I dared not move.

I saw your holy face in death,
    a vision of agony, disfigured,
    stricken by human neglect.

I saw the marks of scorn and insult,
    the dreadful imprint of sin;
    fearsome, this sight of the Lord.

I cried out but no sound came forth;
    ...back in the trap of time,
    spent, breath returned.

II.

The Child of Lisieux saw more in the Holy Face:
    wisdom within the veil of blood and tears,
    treasures to be fathomed in God's embrace
        of distress;

She saw glory there in the pain and torment,
    splendor and salvation in the dark wounds,
    God's thirst for love in the quiet suffering.

She would his immaculate blood become drink
    to purify wayward souls oppressed by sin;
She would we share his thirst to people heaven.

WORDS OF THÉRÈSE – VIII

I would be happy to bear the greatest sufferings – even without God's knowing it, if this were possible – . . . if only I knew that in this way a smile would rise to His lips.

LC-239

When I'm up in heaven, how many graces I will beg for you! Oh! I'll torment God so much that, if He wanted to refuse me at first, my importunity will force Him to grant my desires. This story is in the Gospel.

LC-48

Many things will disappear from heaven because I'll bring them to you. I'll be a little thief; I'll take whatever I please.

LC- 122

God would not have given me the desire of doing good on earth after my death, if he didn't will to realize it. . . . God will have to carry out my will in heaven because I have never done my own will here on earth.

LC-102 / 91

I don't regret giving up my life; but I ask myself: What is this mysterious separation of the soul from the body?

SS-2 6 8

Oh, how little God is loved on this earth, even by priests and religious! No, God isn't loved very much.   LC-139

What beauty? I don't see my beauty at all; I see only the graces I've received from God. You always misunderstand me; you don't know, then, that I'm only a little seedling, a little almond.   LC-144

I cough and cough! I'm just like a locomotive when it arrives at the station; I'm arriving also at a station: heaven, and I'm announcing it.   LC-42

I love you very much, very much! . . . Give me a kiss, a kiss that makes noise; so that the lips go "smack!"   LC 187

Since I'm eating now, I'd really love to have a little chocolate cake, soft inside. . . .it's long, narrow, I believe it's called an éclair. . . . Only one, however!   LC-291

Ah, if I were to forget you, it seems to me that all the saints would chase me out of heaven just as they would an ugly owl. . . .I shall come to take you with me, so that where I am, there also you will be.   LC-66

. . .I must bear with myself such as I am with all my imperfections. But I want to seek out a means of going to heaven by a little way, a way that is very straight, very short, and totally new.   SS-207

. . .it's the way of spiritual childhood, it's the way of confidence and total abandon. I want to teach them the little means that have so perfectly succeeded with me, to tell them there is only one thing to do here on earth: to cast at Jesus the flowers of little sacrifices, . . .this is the way I've taken Him, and it's for this that I shall be so well received.   LC-257

I feel especially that my mission is about to begin, my mission of making God loved as I love Him, of giving my little way to souls. If God answers my requests, my heaven will be spent on earth until the end of the world. Yes, I want to spend my heaven in doing good on earth.

LC-102

. . . When I'm in heaven, I'll draw from God's treasures... you will see; it will be like a shower of roses.   LC-223/62

I have formed such a lofty idea of heaven that, at times, I wonder what God will do at my death to surprise me. . . . if I am not surprised enough, I will pretend to be surprised just to please Him.   LC-43

Ah! but if I go among the Seraphim, I shall not do as they! All of them cover themselves with their wings before God; I will be very careful not to cover myself with my wings.   LC-198

I'm a little seed; no one knows yet what will develop.

LC-103

Oh! it's love! to love, to be loved, and to return to the earth to make love loved.   LC-217

Oh! I love Him! My God, I love you! . . .
                                    [her last words] LC-206

PRAISE AND PETITION

The Lord nurtured her, he guarded her
    as the apple of his eye,
Like a lily, like a rose planted
    near running water.
Prosperity spread over her like a river,
    like a rushing torrent.

> THÉRÈSE,
> BE WITH US WHEN WE ARE WEAK,
> BE WITH US WHEN WE ARE STRONG.

Possessed, a wonder of grace,
    an acceptable offering,
A raging fire of love
    burning in the dark.

> THÉRÈSE,
> BE WITH US WHEN WE DOUBT,
> BE WITH US WHEN SHADOWS COME,
> BE WITH US WHEN LOVE IS NEAR.

CHILDREN LISTEN

Bold, daring, unschooled child;
Bewildered believers savor her words,
Men of mind listen.
Children all,
Listen!

Her words of delight sing of flowers
In darkness among thorns.
A victim of love,
Hear her:

Face the Lord, unfearing,
Trust in the folly
Of his love.

Wisdom's angel,
This child.

Listen!

LIST OF ILLUSTRATIONS